MW01275529

365 / 3
DAYS / YEARS

FINDING THE

Lord

IN ALL THINGS

A *Daily* SPIRITUAL JOURNAL

DESERET
BOOK

SALT LAKE CITY, UTAH

ISBN 978-1-62972-383-9

Printed in China
RR Donnelley, Humen, Guangdong, China

10   9   8   7   6   5   4   3   2   1

◆ ◆ ◆

DID GOD SEND A MESSAGE
that was just for me? Did I see His hand in
my life or the lives of my children? . . . I will
find a way to preserve that memory for
the day that I, and those that I love, will
need to remember how much God loves
us and how much we need Him.

—HENRY B. EYRING,
"O Remember, Remember," *Ensign,*
November 2007, 69.

◆ ◆ ◆

Both ancient and modern-day prophets have encour-
aged the Saints to be a record-keeping people, and yet
life is so busy it can be challenging to find time to write
consistently in a journal.

This journal will help make journaling both quick and
meaningful. With a reflective writing prompt for each day
and a three-year layout to chart your growth, you can learn
to recognize the hand of the Lord in all things while also
preserving memories for you and your family.

1

JANUARY

What is your spiritual goal for the year?
How will you achieve it?

20__ •

20__ •

20__ •

JANUARY

What good things are you
anticipating this year?

2

20__ •

20__ •

20__ •

3

How did you see God's mercy today?

20___ •..

....

....

....

....

20___ •..

....

....

....

....

20___ •..

....

....

....

....

JANUARY

4

How were you compassionate today?

20__ •..

....

....

....

....

20__ •..

....

....

....

....

20__ •..

....

....

....

....

5

JANUARY

Who inspired you today?

20__ •

20__ •

20__ •

JANUARY

6

How were you patient with yourself today?

20__ •

20__ •

20__ •

7

JANUARY

How has a recent prayer been
answered by a song or hymn?

20__ •

20__ •

20__ •

JANUARY

8

How did you show love to your family today?

20___ •...
....
....
....
....

20___ •...
....
....
....
....

20___ •...
....
....
....
....

9

JANUARY

How did you learn by listening
to the Spirit today?

20___ •

20___ •

20___ •

JANUARY

10

How has paying tithing blessed your life?

20__ •
....
....
....
....
....

20__ •
....
....
....
....

20__ •
....
....
....
....
....

11

JANUARY

How were you a disciple of Christ today?

20_ _ •..
....
....
....
....
....

20_ _ •..
....
....
....
....
....

20_ _ •..
....
....
....
....
....

JANUARY

What Christlike attribute do you
want to strengthen? What can you
do to strengthen that attribute?

12

20__ •

20__ •

20__ •

13

JANUARY

What inspired you today?

20_ _ •

20_ _ •

20_ _ •

JANUARY

14

How have the scriptures blessed your life?

20__ •

20__ •

20__ •

15

JANUARY

What was today's best achievement?

20__ •

20__ •

20__ •

JANUARY

How has priesthood power
affected you this week?

16

20__ •

20__ •

20__ •

17

JANUARY

How did you allow God to love you today?

20__ •

20__ •

20__ •

JANUARY

What is something new you
want to try, and why?

18

20__ •

20__ •

20__ •

19

JANUARY

How has serving others blessed you?

20__ •

20__ •

20__ •

JANUARY

20

How can you show God that you trust Him?

20__ •

20__ •

20__ •

21

JANUARY

What are you thankful for today?

20___ •..
....
....
....
....

20___ •..
....
....
....
....

20___ •..
....
....
....
....

JANUARY

22

How did you show courage today?

20__ •

20__ •

20__ •

23

JANUARY

For whom did you pray today?

20___ •

20___ •

20___ •

JANUARY

24

How did the Lord strengthen you today?

20__ •

20__ •

20__ •

25

How did you feel God's love for you today?

20__ •

20__ •

20__ •

JANUARY

26

How can you magnify your calling?

20__ •

....

....

....

....

20__ •

....

....

....

20__ •

....

....

....

....

27

JANUARY

How did you see Heavenly Father's hand
in the creations of the world today?

20_ _ •

20_ _ •

20_ _ •

JANUARY

28

What scripture has touched your life?

20__ •

20__ •

20__ •

29

What tender mercy have you
witnessed in a loved one's life?

20_ _ •

20_ _ •

20_ _ •

JANUARY

How can you show gratitude?

20___ •

20___ •

20___ •

31

JANUARY

What has God done to make
a difference in your life?

20__ •

....

....

....

....

....

20__ •

....

....

....

....

20__ •

....

....

....

....

....

FEBRUARY

What gospel topic is most on
your mind right now?

1

20___ •..

....

....

....

....

20___ •..

....

....

....

....

20___ •..

....

....

....

....

2

FEBRUARY

How has the Atonement of Jesus
Christ blessed your life today?

20__ •

20__ •

20__ •

FEBRUARY

What makes you feel safe?

20__ •

20__ •

20__ •

4

FEBRUARY

What gospel topic did you discuss with
a friend today? What did you learn?

20__ •

20__ •

20__ •

FEBRUARY

5

How did you nourish your faith today?

20___ •

20___ •

20___ •

6

FEBRUARY

How do you honor your parents?

20__ •

20__ •

20__ •

FEBRUARY

7

What brings you joy?

20___ •

20___ •

20___ •

8

FEBRUARY

What or who inspired you today?

20__ •..
....
....
....
....

20__ •..
....
....
....
....

20__ •..
....
....
....
....

FEBRUARY

9

How did the Savior strengthen you today?

20__ •

20__ •

20__ •

10

FEBRUARY

What is one thing you can turn
over to the Lord today?

20__ •..

....

....

....

....

20__ •..

....

....

....

....

20__ •..

....

....

....

....

FEBRUARY

11

How did you care for your body today?

20__ •

20__ •

20__ •

12

FEBRUARY

What gave you comfort today?

20__ •...
....
....
....
....

20__ •...
....
....
....
....

20__ •...
....
....
....
....

FEBRUARY

13

How did you defend your faith today?

20___ •

20___ •

20___ •

14

FEBRUARY

How did you share love today?

20__ •

20__ •

20__ •

FEBRUARY

15

What do you do to feel the Spirit?

20__ •

20__ •

20__ •

16

FEBRUARY

What challenge are you
striving to overcome?

20__ •

20__ •

20__ •

FEBRUARY

17

Whom are you grateful for today?

20__ •

20__ •

20__ •

18

What is your favorite story about Christ?

20__•

20__•

20__•

FEBRUARY

19

What did you pray for today?

20__ •

20__ •

20__ •

20

FEBRUARY

How did you feel Heaven's help today?

20__ •..
....
....
....
....

20__ •..
....
....
....
....

20__ •..
....
....
....
....

FEBRUARY

21

What made you feel happy today?

20__ •

20__ •

20__ •

22

FEBRUARY

Who showed you love today?

20__ •

20__ •

20__ •

FEBRUARY

23

What do you love about yourself?

20__ •

20__ •

20__ •

24

FEBRUARY

How can you shift your priorities
to put God first?

20__ •..

....

....

....

....

20__ •..

....

....

....

....

20__ •..

....

....

....

....

FEBRUARY

What enjoyable thing did you do today?

25

20__ •..

....

....

....

....

20__ •..

....

....

....

....

20__ •..

....

....

....

....

26

FEBRUARY

How has grace touched you today?

20__ •

20__ •

20__ •

FEBRUARY

27

How were you patient today?

20__ •..
....
....
....
....

20__ •..
....
....
....
....

20__ •..
....
....
....
....
....

28

FEBRUARY

What was today's high and low?

20__ •...

....

....

....

....

20__ •...

....

....

....

....

20__ •...

....

....

....

....

MARCH

1

What was the last compliment you gave?

20__ •
....
....
....
....
....

20__ •
....
....
....
....
....

20__ •
....
....
....
....
....

2

MARCH

How did you feel close to God today?

20___ •

20___ •

20___ •

MARCH

How did you follow a prompting
of the Spirit today?

20__ •
....
....
....
....

20__ •
....
....
....
....

20__ •
....
....
....
....

4

MARCH

Which truth do you feel needs to be
defended most in today's world?

20__ •..

....

....

....

....

20__ •..

....

....

....

....

20__ •..

....

....

....

....

MARCH

5

How can you treat yourself more lovingly?

20__ •

20__ •

20__ •

6

How did you let your light shine today?

20__ •

20__ •

20__ •

MARCH

How did you show love for a
family member today?

7

20__ •...
....
....
....
....

20__ •...
....
....
....
....

20__ •...
....
....
....
....

8

MARCH

How were you anxiously engaged
in a good cause today?

20__ •

20__ •

20__ •

MARCH

9

What temptation did you give in to today?

20__ •

20__ •

20__ •

10

MARCH

How did you feel God's grace today?

20__ •

20__ •

20__ •

MARCH

11

How did you show your faith today?

20__ •..

....

....

....

....

20__ •..

....

....

....

....

20__ •..

....

....

....

....

12

What made you grateful today?

20__ •..

....

....

....

....

20__ •..

....

....

....

....

20__ •..

....

....

....

....

MARCH

How did you improve your
relationship with the Lord today?

13

20___ •...

....

....

....

20___ •...

....

....

....

20___ •...

....

....

....

....

14

How does music bring you closer to God?

20__ •..
....
....
....
....
....

20__ •..
....
....
....
....
....

20__ •..
....
....
....
....
....

MARCH

How has the sealing power blessed you?

15

20___ •

20___ •

20___ •

16

MARCH

What brought your family close today?

20__ •

_____

_____

_____

_____

20__ •

_____

_____

_____

_____

20__ •

_____

_____

_____

_____

MARCH

17

Who is a person you admire right now? Why?

20__ •

20__ •

20__ •

18

MARCH

How have you seen the hand
of the Lord in your day?

20__ •...

....

....

....

....

20__ •...

....

....

....

....

20__ •...

....

....

....

....

MARCH

19

What helps you feel God's presence?

20__ •

20__ •

20__ •

20

What change are you currently making
in your life to be more like Christ?

20__ •...
....
....
....
....

20__ •...
....
....
....
....

20__ •...
....
....
....
....

MARCH

21

How has home and/or visiting
teaching blessed you?

20__ •

20__ •

20__ •

22

MARCH

How did you feel the Spirit today?

20__ •

20__ •

20__ •

MARCH

23

How did you show love for a friend today?

20__ •...
....
....
....
....

20__ •...
....
....
....
....

20__ •...
....
....
....
....

24

MARCH

What new gospel insight
did you learn today?

20__ •..
....
....
....
....

20__ •..
....
....
....
....

20__ •..
....
....
....
....

MARCH

How did you support your
church leaders today?

25

20__ •

20__ •

20__ •

26

What distracted you from
following God's will today?

20__ •

20__ •

20__ •

MARCH

27

Which commandment is easiest
for you to live right now?

20__ •..

....

....

....

....

20__ •..

....

....

....

....

20__ •..

....

....

....

....

....

28

MARCH

Which commandment is hardest
for you to live right now?

20__ •

20__ •

20__ •

MARCH

Which of your senses are you
most grateful for today?

29

20__ •

20__ •

20__ •

30

MARCH

What surprised you today?

20__ •..
....
....
....
....
....

20__ •..
....
....
....
....
....

20__ •..
....
....
....
....
....

MARCH

31

How are your children or your
parents a blessing to you?

20__ •..
....
....
....
....

20__ •..
....
....
....
....

20__ •..
....
....
....
....

1

APRIL

How has the Lord answered
your prayers today?

20__ •..
....
....
....
....
....

20__ •..
....
....
....
....
....

20__ •..
....
....
....
....
....

APRIL

2

How were you a blessing to someone else?

20__ •

20__ •

20__ •

3

APRIL

How do you participate in
general conference?

20__ •...
....
....
....
....

20__ •...
....
....
....
....

20__ •...
....
....
....
....

APRIL

4

How did you sustain the prophet today?

20__ •

20__ •

20__ •

5

APRIL

What talk resonated with you during
this general conference?

20__ •

20__ •

20__ •

APRIL

How did you share your testimony
of the restored gospel today?

20___ •

20___ •

20___ •

7

APRIL

What wise choice did you make today?

20__ •

20__ •

20__ •

APRIL

How does the Lord speak to you?

8

20___ •

20___ •

20___ •

9

APRIL

What will you change or improve as
a result of general conference?

20__ •

20__ •

20__ •

APRIL

10

How were you part of a family today?

20___ •

20___ •

20___ •

11

APRIL

What evidence of God's mercy
did you see today?

20___ •...

....

....

....

....

20___ •...

....

....

....

....

20___ •...

....

....

....

....

APRIL

What is a gospel doctrine
that you wrestle with?

12

20__ •

20__ •

20__ •

13

APRIL

How did you follow a (past or present) prophet today?

20__ •

20__ •

20__ •

APRIL

How did you stand as a
witness of God today?

14

20__ •

20__ •

20__ •

15

APRIL

Why are you grateful for
eternal families today?

20__ •

20__ •

20__ •

APRIL

How has your knowledge of the plan
of salvation influenced your day?

20__ •

20__ •

20__ •

17

APRIL

How did you honor your
baptismal covenant today?

20__ •...
....
....
....
....

20__ •...
....
....
....
....

20__ •...
....
....
....
....

APRIL

18

How do you show mercy to others?

20__ •

....

....

....

....

20__ •

....

....

....

....

20__ •

....

....

....

....

19

APRIL

What is one thing you were
prompted to do today?

20__ •

20__ •

20__ •

APRIL

20

How did the Lord strengthen you today?

20___ •

20___ •

20___ •

21

APRIL

What was your favorite thing about today?

20__ •

20__ •

20__ •

APRIL

What spiritual gift are you
developing right now?

22

20__ •

20__ •

20__ •

23

What gives you hope?

20__ •

20__ •

20__ •

APRIL

What do you find yourself
returning to again and again?

20__ •

20__ •

20__ •

25

What matters most to you right now?

20__ •

20__ •

20__ •

APRIL

What caused you to think
of the Savior today?

26

20__ •

20__ •

20__ •

27

How did you serve the Lord today?

20__ •

20__ •

20__ •

APRIL

28

What is one thing you can stop—or give up—that will draw you closer to the Lord?

20__ •

20__ •

20__ •

29

APRIL

What decision did you make today
that will affect your future?

20___ •..

....

....

....

....

20___ •..

....

....

....

....

20___ •..

....

....

....

....

APRIL

What inspired you today?

30

20__ •

20__ •

20__ •

1

MAY

How has the law of the fast blessed your life?

20___ •

20___ •

20___ •

MAY

How did you lift someone else today?

2

20__ •
....
....
....
....

20__ •
....
....
....
....

20__ •
....
....
....
....

3

MAY

What is something you need to "just do"?

20___ •

20___ •

20___ •

MAY

4

How can you be more in tune with the Spirit?

20__ •..
....
....
....
....

20__ •..
....
....
....
....

20__ •..
....
....
....
....

5

What did you pray for today?

20__ •

20__ •

20__ •

MAY

6

How did you follow the Spirit today?

20__ •

20__ •

20__ •

7

MAY

How did you practice charity today?

20__ •

20__ •

20__ •

MAY

8

How were you a little better today?

20__ •

20__ •

20__ •

9

MAY

What is something great you have done?

20__ •

20__ •

20__ •

MAY

How do you share the gospel with others?

10

20__ •

20__ •

20__ •

11

What made you laugh today?

20__ •..
....
....
....
....

20__ •..
....
....
....
....

20__ •..
....
....
....
....

MAY

12

What is stopping you from moving forward?

20__ •
....
....
....
....

20__ •
....
....
....
....

20__ •
....
....
....
....
....

13

How has God's grace enabled you?

20__ •

20__ •

20__ •

MAY

14

What is one thing your mother taught you?

20__ •

20__ •

20__ •

15

MAY

How did the Lord warn you today?

20___ •

20___ •

20___ •

MAY

16

How do you keep the Sabbath day holy?

20__ •
....
....
....
....

20__ •
....
....
....
....

20__ •
....
....
....
....

17

What have you done that is difficult?

20__ •...
....
....
....
....

20__ •...
....
....
....
....

20__ •...
....
....
....
....

MAY

18

How did you control your thoughts today?

20__ •

20__ •

20__ •

19

MAY

How were you selfless today?

20__ •

20__ •

20__ •

MAY

How did you build your testimony today?

20

20___ •

20___ •

20___ •

21

MAY

What was the last compliment you gave?

20__ •

20__ •

20__ •

MAY

What gospel topic are you
studying right now?

22

20__ •

20__ •

20__ •

23

MAY

How did the knowledge that you are a child of God influence your actions today?

20 __ •

20 __ •

20 __ •

MAY

24

How did you follow Christ's example today?

20__ •

20__ •

20__ •

25

MAY

What has recently helped you
strengthen your own faith?

20__ •

20__ •

20__ •

MAY

26

What is a good habit you have developed?

20__ •
....
....
....
....

20__ •
....
....
....
....

20__ •
....
....
....
....

27 ——————————— MAY

What was the last thing you fasted for?

20__ •..
....
....
....
....

20__ •..
....
....
....
....

20__ •..
....
....
....
....

MAY

28

How did you brighten the world today?

20__ •
....
....
....
....
....

20__ •
....
....
....
....
....

20__ •
....
....
....
....
....

29

MAY

How did you share your love
for someone today?

20__ •..

....

....

....

....

20__ •..

....

....

....

....

20__ •..

....

....

....

....

MAY

How was a prayer answered today?

30

20__ •

20__ •

20__ •

31

Which blessing are you still waiting for?

20__ •

20__ •

20__ •

JUNE

1

When have you witnessed God's timing?

20__ •
....
....
....
....
....

20__ •
....
....
....
....
....

20__ •
....
....
....
....
....

2

JUNE

What is a doctrine or gospel truth that you love?

20__ •

20__ •

20__ •

JUNE

How did you feel strengthened
by the Lord today?

3

20__ •..
....
....
....
....

20__ •..
....
....
....
....

20__ •..
....
....
....
....

4

JUNE

How do you focus on the
ordinance of the sacrament?

20___ •

20___ •

20___ •

JUNE

What question are you
seeking an answer for?

5

20___ •..
....
....
....
....

20___ •..
....
....
....
....

20___ •..
....
....
....
....

6

JUNE

How did you make your life joyful today?

20__ •
....
....
....
....
....

20__ •
....
....
....
....
....

20__ •
....
....
....
....
....

JUNE

What miracle, large or small,
have you seen in your life?

7

20__ •

20__ •

20__ •

8

JUNE

Who inspired you today?

20__ •

20__ •

20__ •

JUNE

Which of your worries can
you give to the Lord?

20_____ •

20_____ •

20_____ •

9

10

JUNE

Who showed you loving kindness today?

20__ •..
....
....
....
....

20__ •..
....
....
....
....

20__ •..
....
....
....
....

JUNE

11

How did you interact with nature today?

20__ •

20__ •

20__ •

12

JUNE

How does the Spirit
communicate with you?

20__ •

20__ •

20__ •

JUNE

13

How were you patient in your trials today?

20__ •

20__ •

20__ •

14

JUNE

What was the highlight of today?

20__ •

20__ •

20__ •

JUNE

How can you make more room
for Jesus in your life?

15

20__ •

20__ •

20__ •

16

JUNE

How did you follow Christ's example today?

20__ •..
....
....
....
....
....

20__ •..
....
....
....
....
....

20__ •..
....
....
....
....
....

JUNE

17

How can you love another more completely?

20___ •..
....
....
....
....

20___ •..
....
....
....
....

20___ •..
....
....
....
....

18

JUNE

What is one thing your father taught you?

20__ •..
....
....
....
....

20__ •..
....
....
....
....

20__ •..
....
....
....
....

JUNE

What did you do today that you
can do better tomorrow?

19

20__ •

20__ •

20__ •

20

JUNE

What gave you comfort today?

20__ •...
....
....
....
....

20__ •...
....
....
....
....

20__ •...
....
....
....
....

JUNE

What do you wish you had more time to do?

21

20__ •

20__ •

20__ •

22

JUNE

How did you seek the Savior today?

20__ •...
....
....
....
....
....

20__ •...
....
....
....
....
....

20__ •...
....
....
....
....
....

JUNE

How have your decisions
affected someone else?

23

20___ •

20___ •

20___ •

24

JUNE

How were you a missionary today?

20__ •...

....

....

....

....

20__ •...

....

....

....

....

20__ •...

....

....

....

....

JUNE

What's something you haven't succeeded
at yet, but keep trying to accomplish?

25

20__ •

20__ •

20__ •

26

How has service blessed your life?

20__ •

20__ •

20__ •

JUNE

27

What is a worry you can cast on the Lord?

20__ •..
....
....
....

20__ •..
....
....
....

20__ •..
....
....
....

28

JUNE

What made you smile today?

20__ •...
....
....
....
....
....

20__ •...
....
....
....
....
....

20__ •...
....
....
....
....
....

JUNE

29

How has grace touched your day?

20__ •

20__ •

20__ •

30

What did you struggle with today?

20__ •
....
....
....
....

20__ •
....
....
....
....

20__ •
....
....
....
....

JULY

How did you act on your faith today?

1

20___ •

20___ •

20___ •

2

JULY

What were you thankful for today?

20___•..
....
....
....
....

20___•..
....
....
....
....

20___•..
....
....
....
....

JULY

3

What challenges did you take
to the Lord today?

20___ •..
....
....
....
....

20___ •..
....
....
....
....

20___ •..
....
....
....
....

4

JULY

How did you show gratitude
for your freedoms today?

20__ •

20__ •

20__ •

JULY

How do you share the Lord's
goodness with others?

5

20__ •

20__ •

20__ •

6

JULY

How did you step out of your
comfort zone today?

20__ •..

....

....

....

....

20__ •..

....

....

....

....

20__ •..

....

....

....

....

JULY

7

What was the focus of your prayers today?

20__ •
....

....

....

....

20__ •
....

....

....

....

20__ •
....

....

....

....

8

JULY

How did the Atonement bless you today?

20__ •..
....
....
....
....

20__ •..
....
....
....
....

20__ •..
....
....
....
....

JULY

What made you smile today?

9

20___ •

20___ •

20___ •

10

What scripture influenced your day?

20___ •

20___ •

20___ •

JULY

How were you willing to
serve the Lord today?

11

20__ •...
....
....
....

20__ •...
....
....
....

20__ •...
....
....
....

12

JULY

In what ways can you simplify your life?

20__ •..
....
....
....
....

20__ •..
....
....
....
....

20__ •..
....
....
....
....

JULY

13

Who showed love for you today?

20__ •

20__ •

20__ •

14

How did your faith help solve
a problem today?

20___ •..
....
....
....
....
....

20___ •..
....
....
....
....
....

20___ •..
....
....
....
....
....

JULY

What unasked-for blessing
did you notice today?

20__ •

20__ •

20__ •

16

JULY

How did you serve someone today?

20__ •

20__ •

20__ •

JULY

17

What made you feel excited today?

20___ •

20___ •

20___ •

18

JULY

How did you stand for truth today?

20__ •

20__ •

20__ •

JULY

19

What makes you feel loved?

20__ •

20__ •

20__ •

20

JULY

What do you most want to improve?

20__ •

20__ •

20__ •

JULY

21

How did you study the gospel today?

20__ •

20__ •

20__ •

22

JULY

How can you exercise
gentleness in your life?

20__ •

20__ •

20__ •

JULY

How do you know that the Savior loves you?

23

20__ •

20__ •

20__ •

24

How can you be a pioneer for the gospel?

20__ •

20__ •

20__ •

JULY

25

What did you give to the Lord today?

20___ •..

....

....

....

....

20___ •..

....

....

....

....

20___ •..

....

....

....

....

26

How did you praise God today?

20__ •

20__ •

20__ •

JULY

27

What service did you perform today?

20__ •

20__ •

20__ •

28

JULY

How were you tempted today?

20__ •..
....
....
....
....
....

20__ •..
....
....
....
....
....

20__ •..
....
....
....
....
....

JULY

How does the Holy Ghost give
you comfort and peace?

29

20__ •

20__ •

20__ •

30

JULY

If today were your last day,
what would you do?

20___ •...

....

....

....

....

....

20___ •...

....

....

....

....

....

20___ •...

....

....

....

....

....

JULY

31

What is one of your happiest memories?

20___ •

20___ •

20___ •

1

AUGUST

How did you invite the Spirit into your day?

20__ •

20__ •

20__ •

AUGUST

2

How can you be a peacemaker in your life?

20__ •

20__ •

20__ •

3

How did you show love for yourself today?

20 _ _ •

20 _ _ •

20 _ _ •

AUGUST

4

How did you use your agency today?

20___ •

20___ •

20___ •

5

AUGUST

Whom did you pray for today?

20__ •...
....
....
....
....

20__ •...
....
....
....
....

20__ •...
....
....
....
....

AUGUST

How did you remember your
covenants today?

20__ •

20__ •

20__ •

7

AUGUST

Who needs your unconditional love?

20__ •..

....

....

....

....

20__ •..

....

....

....

....

20__ •..

....

....

....

....

AUGUST

8

How did you share your testimony today?

20__ •

20__ •

20__ •

9

AUGUST

To whom did you show love
and kindness today?

20__ •..
....
....
....
....

20__ •..
....
....
....
....

20__ •..
....
....
....
....

AUGUST

What was the best thing that
happened today?

20___ •

20___ •

20___ •

11

How did you feel close to God today?

20__ •..

....

....

....

....

20__ •..

....

....

....

....

20__ •..

....

....

....

....

AUGUST

What secret act of service
did you give today?

12

20___ •

20___ •

20___ •

13

AUGUST

What was the focus of your thoughts today?

20__ •

20__ •

20__ •

AUGUST

14

How were your prayers answered today?

20__ •

20__ •

20__ •

15

AUGUST

What are the most significant battles
you are currently fighting?

20___ •..
....
....
....
....

20___ •..
....
....
....
....

20___ •..
....
....
....
....

AUGUST

What did you feel today that tells
you the Lord loves you?

16

20__ •..

....

....

....

....

20__ •..

....

....

....

....

20__ •..

....

....

....

....

17

AUGUST

How did you see the Lord's love
in someone else's life today?

20___ •

20___ •

20___ •

AUGUST

18

How did you seek forgiveness today?

20__ •

....
....
....
....

20__ •

....
....
....
....

20__ •

....
....
....
....

19

AUGUST

How has a friend blessed your life today?

20__ •..
....
....
....
....

20__ •..
....
....
....
....

20__ •..
....
....
....
....

AUGUST

What was your scripture
study about today?

20

20__ •

20__ •

20__ •

21

AUGUST

What did you discuss in family
council this week?

20__ •

20__ •

20__ •

AUGUST

22

How has following God blessed you?

20__ •

20__ •

20__ •

23

AUGUST

What made you grateful today?

20__ •

20__ •

20__ •

AUGUST

24

How was your attitude today?

20__ •

20__ •

20__ •

25

AUGUST

How has your heart been turned to
your fathers and your children?

20__ •

20__ •

20__ •

AUGUST

What small thing did you do
today to share the gospel?

26

20__ •

20__ •

20__ •

27

How do you show reverence?

20__ •

20__ •

20__ •

AUGUST

What's something for which you
need to forgive yourself?

28

20__ •

20__ •

20__ •

29

AUGUST

How has taking the sacrament
weekly blessed you?

20__ •

20__ •

20__ •

AUGUST

30

How did the Savior strengthen you today?

20__ •

20__ •

20__ •

31

AUGUST

Where did you study the scriptures today?

20__ •..

....

....

....

....

20__ •..

....

....

....

....

20__ •..

....

....

....

....

....

SEPTEMBER

1

How did you choose the right today?

20__ •

20__ •

20__ •

2

SEPTEMBER

How were you "anxiously engaged
in a good cause" today?

20__ •

20__ •

20__ •

SEPTEMBER

What is one of your favorite
stories from Church history?

3

20__ •..

....

....

....

....

20__ •..

....

....

....

....

20__ •..

....

....

....

....

4

SEPTEMBER

How did you stand as a
witness of God today?

20__ •..
....
....
....
....
....

20__ •..
....
....
....
....
....

20__ •..
....
....
....
....
....

SEPTEMBER

5

What is one stumbling block in your life?

20__ •

20__ •

20__ •

SEPTEMBER

How did you "put off the natural man" today?

20__ •
....
....
....
....
....

20__ •
....
....
....
....
....

20__ •
....
....
....
....
....

SEPTEMBER

How are you contributing to
the gathering of Israel?

7

20__ •

20__ •

20__ •

8

SEPTEMBER

How has the priesthood blessed you?

20__ •...
....
....
....
....

20__ •...
....
....
....
....

20__ •...
....
....
....
....

SEPTEMBER

9

How do you treat your body like a temple?

20__ •

20__ •

20__ •

10

SEPTEMBER

What have you learned from your
grandparents or ancestors?

20__ •

20__ •

20__ •

SEPTEMBER

Whom did you see helping
someone else today?

11

20__ •

20__ •

20__ •

12

SEPTEMBER

What in the gospel requires "work" for you?

20__ •

20__ •

20__ •

SEPTEMBER

13

How can you be more obedient?

20___ •

20___ •

20___ •

14

SEPTEMBER

What correction or chastisement
are you grateful for?

20__ •

20__ •

20__ •

SEPTEMBER

What is a spiritual gift you
would like to develop?

20__ •

20__ •

20__ •

16

What did you learn about God today?

20__ •..
....
....
....
....
....

20__ •..
....
....
....
....
....

20__ •..
....
....
....
....
....

SEPTEMBER

Which of God's creations are you
most inspired by today?

17

20__ •

20__ •

20__ •

18

SEPTEMBER

How have you felt God's grace in your life?.

20__ •...
....
....
....
....

20__ •...
....
....
....
....

20__ •...
....
....
....
....

SEPTEMBER

19

What made you feel happy today?

20__ •
....
....
....
....

20__ •
....
....
....
....

20__ •
....
....
....
....

20

SEPTEMBER

What fears can you work on mastering?

20__ •

20__ •

20__ •

SEPTEMBER

How have you exercised self-control
(or self-discipline) today?

21

20__ •

20__ •

20__ •

22

SEPTEMBER

How has the missionary program
blessed your life?

20__ •...
....
....
....
....

20__ •...
....
....
....
....

20__ •...
....
....
....
....

SEPTEMBER

23

What has the prophet said recently
that has influenced your life?

20__ •..

....

....

....

20__ •..

....

....

....

20__ •..

....

....

....

....

24

SEPTEMBER

Which hymn or Primary song
is your current favorite?

20__ •..
....
....
....
....
....

20__ •..
....
....
....
....
....

20__ •..
....
....
....
....
....

SEPTEMBER

How was your testimony of Jesus
Christ strengthened today?

25

20__ •

20__ •

20__ •

26

SEPTEMBER

How did you feel close to God today?

20__ •..

....

....

....

....

20__ •..

....

....

....

....

20__ •..

....

....

....

....

....

SEPTEMBER

27

How can you accept yourself more fully?

20__ •

20__ •

20__ •

28

SEPTEMBER

What enemy do you need to pray for?

20__ •

20__ •

20__ •

SEPTEMBER

Why are you grateful for the
Book of Mormon today?

29

20__ •

20__ •

20__ •

30

SEPTEMBER

What guidance are you seeking
from general conference?

20__ •

20__ •

20__ •

OCTOBER

What good habit are you
striving to develop?

20___ •

20___ •

20___ •

2

OCTOBER

How did you follow the counsel
of the prophets today?

20__ •

20__ •

20__ •

OCTOBER

3

How has the temple blessed your life?

20___ •

20___ •

20___ •

4

OCTOBER

How can you help the needy?

20___ •

20___ •

20___ •

OCTOBER

5

What was your favorite thing about today?

20__ •..

....

....

....

....

20__ •..

....

....

....

....

20__ •..

....

....

....

....

OCTOBER

Which talk or theme stood out to
you in general conference?

20__ •

....

....

....

....

....

20__ •

....

....

....

....

....

20__ •

....

....

....

....

....

OCTOBER

7

How do you uphold religious liberty?

20__ •..

....

....

....

....

20__ •..

....

....

....

....

20__ •..

....

....

....

....

8

OCTOBER

How has the Primary program blessed you?

20__ •..
....
....
....
....
....

20__ •..
....
....
....
....
....

20__ •..
....
....
....
....
....

OCTOBER

9

How were you a missionary today?

20__ •

20__ •

20__ •

10

OCTOBER

What did you do in your last
family home evening?

20___ •...

....

....

....

....

20___ •...

....

....

....

....

20___ •...

....

....

....

....

OCTOBER

11

What did you study in the scriptures today?

20__ •

....

....

....

....

20__ •

....

....

....

....

20__ •

....

....

....

....

....

12

OCTOBER

How did you soften your heart today?

20__ •...
....
....
....
....

20__ •...
....
....
....
....

20__ •...
....
....
....
....

OCTOBER

How does your family like to
spend time together?

13

20__ •

20__ •

20__ •

14

Which talents or attributes would
you like to have or improve?

20_ _ •..

....

....

....

....

20_ _ •..

....

....

....

....

20_ _ •..

....

....

....

....

OCTOBER

15

Who showed you mercy today?

20__ •
....
....
....
....

20__ •
....
....
....
....

20__ •
....
....
....
....
....

16

OCTOBER

How does your knowledge of the plan of salvation affect your choices today?

20__ •..

....

....

....

....

20__ •..

....

....

....

....

20__ •..

....

....

....

....

OCTOBER

17

How have eternal families blessed you?

20__ •

20__ •

20__ •

18

OCTOBER

How have you seen the light of
Christ in your life today?

20__ •

20__ •

20__ •

OCTOBER

19

How did you exercise wisdom today?

20__ •

20__ •

20__ •

20

OCTOBER

What gospel insights have
you learned recently?

20__ •...
....
....
....
....
....

20__ •...
....
....
....
....
....

20__ •...
....
....
....
....
....

OCTOBER

21

How did you strengthen your family today?

20__ •

20__ •

20__ •

22

OCTOBER

What challenge are you
striving to overcome?

20__ •

20__ •

20__ •

OCTOBER

23

Which book has brought you closer to God?

20__ •

20__ •

20__ •

24

OCTOBER

Who served you today?

20__ •

20__ •

20__ •

OCTOBER

25

What did you pray about today?

20__ •..
....
....
....
....

20__ •..
....
....
....
....

20__ •..
....
....
....
....

26

What are you working on that will
bring you closer to Christ?

20__ •

20__ •

20__ •

OCTOBER

Who or what gave you a better
perspective today?

27

20__ •

20__ •

20__ •

28

OCTOBER

What gospel topic would you
like to learn more about?

20__ •

20__ •

20__ •

OCTOBER

29

How did technology help you to learn
and apply the gospel today?

20__ •

20__ •

20__ •

30

OCTOBER

How has paying tithing
blessed you recently?

20__ •...

....

....

....

....

20__ •...

....

....

....

....

20__ •...

....

....

....

....

....

OCTOBER

31

Why are you grateful for
eternal families today?

20__ •

20__ •

20__ •

1

NOVEMBER

What did you do to feel the Spirit today?

20__ •..
....
....
....
....

20__ •..
....
....
....
....

20__ •..
....
....
....
....

NOVEMBER

How did you express gratitude today?

2

20___ •

20___ •

20___ •

3

NOVEMBER

How did you go the extra mile today?

20__ •..
....
....
....
....

20__ •..
....
....
....
....

20__ •..
....
....
....
....

NOVEMBER

4

How did Christ grant you peace today?

20__ •

20__ •

20__ •

5

NOVEMBER

What have you learned from serving
in your current church calling?

20__ •

20__ •

20__ •

NOVEMBER

What tender mercy did you
receive from the Lord today?

20___ •

20___ •

20___ •

7

NOVEMBER

For whom did you do something kind today?

20__ •

20__ •

20__ •

NOVEMBER

8

How could you magnify your current calling?

20__ •

20__ •

20__ •

9

With whom did you share your time today?

20__ •...
....
....
....
....

20__ •...
....
....
....
....

20__ •...
....
....
....
....

NOVEMBER

10

How are you building Zion in your life?

20__ •

20__ •

20__ •

11

NOVEMBER

How did you "obey, honor, and
sustain" the law today?

20__ •

20__ •

20__ •

NOVEMBER

12

How is faith influencing your life?

20__ •

20__ •

20__ •

13

NOVEMBER

How did you build your character today?

20__ •

20__ •

20__ •

NOVEMBER

14

What or who gave you hope today?

20__ •

20__ •

20__ •

15

NOVEMBER

How did you use your talents to
uplift those around you today?

20__ •

20__ •

20__ •

NOVEMBER

How did God help you achieve
something today?

16

20__ •

20__ •

20__ •

17

NOVEMBER

What negative practice or habit
have you conquered?

20__ •

20__ •

20__ •

NOVEMBER

What gospel topic or scripture
did you ponder today?

18

20___ •

20___ •

20___ •

19

NOVEMBER

How did you use your time wisely today?

20__ •

20__ •

20__ •

NOVEMBER

20

Why are you grateful for your body today?

20__ •

20__ •

20__ •

21

NOVEMBER

What did you learn in Sunday
School this week?

20__ •...

....

....

....

....

20__ •...

....

....

....

....

20__ •...

....

....

....

....

NOVEMBER

What prompting or insight did the
Holy Ghost give you today?

22

20__ •

20__ •

20__ •

23

NOVEMBER

What did you think about most today?

20__ •..

....

....

....

....

20__ •..

....

....

....

....

20__ •..

....

....

....

....

NOVEMBER

What distracted you from
your purpose today?

24

20__ •

20__ •

20__ •

25

NOVEMBER

What are you most thankful for?

20__ • ....
....
....
....
....
....

20__ • ....
....
....
....
....

20__ • ....
....
....
....
....
....

NOVEMBER

26

What spiritual goal are you working on?

20__ •

20__ •

20__ •

27

NOVEMBER

How did you set a good example today?

20__ •

20__ •

20__ •

NOVEMBER

28

What gave you comfort today?

20___ •

20___ •

20___ •

29

NOVEMBER

What temporal goal are you
working on right now?

20__ •

20__ •

20__ •

NOVEMBER

30

How did faith guide you today?

20__ •

20__ •

20__ •

1

DECEMBER

What was your scripture study about today?

20__ •...
....
....
....
....

20__ •...
....
....
....
....

20__ •...
....
....
....
....

DECEMBER

2

How did you improve a relationship today?

20__ •

20__ •

20__ •

3

DECEMBER

How did you follow the 13th
Article of Faith today?

20__ •

20__ •

20__ •

DECEMBER

4

Whom did you serve today?

20___ •
....
....
....
....

20___ •
....
....
....
....

20___ •
....
....
....
....

5

DECEMBER

What has recently helped you
strengthen your own faith?

20__ •...

....

....

....

....

20__ •...

....

....

....

....

20__ •...

....

....

....

....

DECEMBER

Which gospel principle or spiritual prompting
influenced your actions today?

6

20__ •

....

....

....

....

20__ •

....

....

....

....

20__ •

....

....

....

....

7

DECEMBER

What small act of kindness did
you show someone today?

20__ •

20__ •

20__ •

DECEMBER

8

How did you feel God's love for you today?

20__ •

20__ •

20__ •

9

How was a prayer answered today?

20___ •...

....

....

....

....

....

20___ •...

....

....

....

....

....

20___ •...

....

....

....

....

....

DECEMBER

How do you reflect on Christ
during the holiday season?

20__ •

20__ •

20__ •

11

DECEMBER

How has humility brought you
closer to the Savior?

20___ •

20___ •

20___ •

DECEMBER

What weakness did God help
you overcome today?

12

20__ •

20__ •

20__ •

13

DECEMBER

How did someone make you smile today?

20__ •..
....
....
....
....
....

20__ •..
....
....
....
....
....

20__ •..
....
....
....
....
....

DECEMBER

14

How did you look outside yourself today?

20___ •

20___ •

20___ •

15

DECEMBER

How can you become a better
version of yourself?

20__ •

20__ •

20__ •

DECEMBER

16

How did you choose eternal life today?

20__ •

20__ •

20__ •

17

DECEMBER

How did you yield to the Spirit today?

20__ •

20__ •

20__ •

DECEMBER

What gift will you give to
the Savior this year?

18

20___ •

20___ •

20___ •

19

DECEMBER

How have your covenants empowered you?

20__ •

20__ •

20__ •

DECEMBER

How have you shown love
for your family today?

20

20__ •

20__ •

20__ •

21

How has the influence of little
children blessed your life?

20__ •..

....

....

....

....

20__ •..

....

....

....

....

20__ •..

....

....

....

....

....

DECEMBER

What caused you to "rejoice
in Christ" today?

22

20__ •

20__ •

20__ •

23

DECEMBER

Why are you grateful for the life and mission of Joseph Smith today?

20___ •

20___ •

20___ •

DECEMBER

What did you do to feel
closer to Christ today?

24

20___ •

20___ •

20___ •

25

DECEMBER

What did you do to celebrate
the birth of Christ today?

20___ •

20___ •

20___ •

DECEMBER

26

How has service blessed your life?

20__ •

20__ •

20__ •

27

DECEMBER

What is one thing you can give up to draw closer to the Savior today?

20__ •..
....
....
....
....

20__ •..
....
....
....
....

20__ •..
....
....
....
....

DECEMBER

28

What gospel theme spoke
most to you this year?

20__ •

20__ •

20__ •

29

DECEMBER

What was your proudest moment this year?

20__ •

20__ •

20__ •

DECEMBER

30

How have you improved over the past year?

20__ •

20__ •

20__ •

31

DECEMBER

What are your hopes and dreams
for the upcoming year?

20__ •..
....
....
....
....

20__ •..
....
....
....
....

20__ •..
....
....
....
....